Computer fundamental

UNIT: 1 INTRODUCTION TO COMPUTER

1. WHAT IS COMPUTER?

- The word "computer" is comes from the word "TO COMPUTE" means to calculate.
- A computer is normally considered to be a calculation device which can perform the arithmetic operations very speedily.
- A computer may be defined as a device which operates upon the data.
- Data can be in the form of numbers, letters, symbols, size etc. And it comes in various shapes & sizes depending upon the type of computer application.
- <u>A computer can store, process & retrieve data as and when we desired.</u>
- The fact that computer process data is so fundamental that many people have started calling as "Data Processor".
- A computer first it gets the Data, does Process on it and then produces Information.

- <u>DEFINATION OF COMPUTER</u>
  - A computer is an electronic device which takes input from the user, processes it and gives the output as per user's requirement.
  - So the main tasks of performed by the computer are:
    - Input
    - Process
    - Output

2. WRITE DOWN THE CHARACTERISTICS OF COMPUTER

Some important characteristics of the computer are as follow:

- Automatic:
  - Computers are automatic machines because it works by itself without human intervention.
  - Once it started on a job they carry on until the job is finished.
  - Computer cannot start themselves.

- They can works from the instructions which are stored inside the system in the form of programs which specify how a particular job is to be done.
- **Accuracy:**
  - The accuracy of a computer is very high.
  - The degree of accuracy of a particular computer depends upon its design.
  - Errors can occur by the computer. But these are due to human weakness, due to incorrect data, but not due to the technological weakness.
- **Speed:**
  - Computer is a very fact device. It can perform the amount of work in few seconds for which a human can take an entire year.
  - While talking about computer speed we do not talk in terms of seconds and milliseconds but in microseconds.
  - A powerful computer is capable of performing several billion (10^9) simple arithmetic operations per second.
- **Diligence:**
  - Unlike human beings, a computer is free from monotony, tiredness & lack of concentration.
  - It can continuously work for hours without creating any error & without grumbling.
  - If you give ten million calculations to performed, it will perform with exactly the same accuracy & speed as the first one.
- **Versatility:**
  - It is one of the most wonderful features about the computer.
  - One moment it is preparing the results of a particular examination, the next moment it is busy with preparing electricity bills and in between it may be helping an office secretary to trace an important letter in seconds.
- **Power of remembering:**
  - Computer can store and recall any amount of data because of its high storage capacity of its storage devices.
  - Every piece of information can be retained as long as desired by the user and can be recalled as and when required.
  - Even after several years, if the information recalled, it will be as accurate as on the day when it was filled to the computers.
- **No I.Q.**
  - A computer is not a magical device; it processes no intelligence of its own.
  - Its I.Q. is zero.

- It has to be told what to do & in what sequence.
- It cannot take its own decision.

- **No Fallings:**
  - A Computer has no feelings because they are machines.
  - Based on our feelings, task, knowledge and experience we often make certain judgments in our day today life.
  - But Computer goes exactly the way which we have given the instructions.

3. EXPLAIN THE DATA PROCESSING CYCLE OF COMPUTER.

- The computer Data Processing is any process that a computer program does to enter data & summarise, analyse or convert data into useable information.
- The process may be automated & run on a computer.
- It involves recording, analysing, storing, summarising & storing data.
- Because data are most useful when it is well presented & informative.

The Data Processing Cycle:

- Data Processing cycle described all activities which are common to all data processing systems from manual to electronic systems.
- These activities can be grouped in four functional categories, viz., data input, data processing, data output and storage, constituting what is known as a data processing cycle.
- The main aim of data processing cycle is to convert the data into meaningful information.
- Data processing system are often referred to as Information System.
- The Information System typically take raw Data as Input to produce Information as Output.

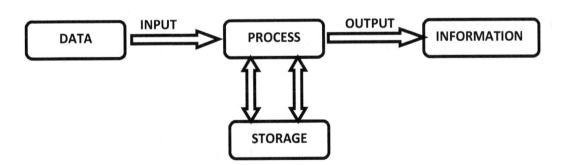

- The data processing cycle contains main four functions:
  - Data input

3

- o **Data process**
- o **Data storage**
- o **Data output**
- **DATA INPUT**
  - o The term input refers to the activities required to record data.
  - o It's a process to entered data in to computer system.
  - o So before we input any data, it is necessary to check or verify the data context.
- **DATA PROCESSING**
  - o The term processing includes the activities like classifying, storing, calculating, comparing or summarising the data.
  - o The processing means to use techniques to convert the data into meaningful information.
- **DATA OUTPUT**
  - o It's a communication function which transmits the information to the outside world.
  - o After completed the process the data are converted into the meaningful in
  - o Sometimes the output also includes the decoding activity which converts the electronically generated information into human readable form.
- **DATA STORAGE**
  - o It involves the filling of data & information for future use.

4. EXPLAIN THE CLASSIFICATION OF THE COMPUTER BY DATA PROCESSED

The computers are divided mainly three types on the based on data processed:

1. Analog computers
2. Digital computers
3. Hybrid computers

Analog computers:

- In Analog Computers, data is represented as continuously varying voltage and operate essentially by measuring rather counting.
- As the data is continuously variable, the results obtained are estimated and not exactly repeatable.
- It can able to perform multiple tasks simultaneously and also capable to work effectively with the irrational number. E.g. $1/8 = 0.125$ and $1/6 = 0.1666$

- Voltage, temperature and pressure are measured using analog devices like voltmeters, thermometers and barometers.

Digital Computers

- The digit computer is a machine based on digital technology which represents information by numerical digit.
- In Digital Computers data is represented as discrete units of electrical pulses. The data is measured in quantities represented as either the 'on' or 'off' state.
- Therefore, the results obtained from a digital computer are accurate.
- Virtually all of today's computers are based on digital computers.

Hybrid Computers

- It combines the good features of both analog & digital computers.
- It has a speed of analog computer & accuracy of digital computer.
- Hybrid Computers accept data in analog form and present output also in digitally.
- The data however is processed digitally.
- Therefore, hybrid computers require analog-to-digital and digital-to-analog converters for output.

5. EXPLAIN THE CLASSIFICATION OF THE COMPUTER BY DATA PROCESSING:

The computers are classified in four types on the based on data processing.

- Micro computer
- Mini computer
- Mainframe computer
- Super computer

Micro Computer:

- Micro computers are the computers with having a microprocessor chip as it central processing unit.
- Originated in late 1970s.
- First micro computer was built with 8 bit processor.
- Microcomputer is known as personal computer.
- Designed to use by individual whether in the form of pc's, workstation or notebook computers.
- Small in size and affordable for general people.
- Ex: IBM PC, IBM PC/XT, IBM PC/AT

Micro Computer:

- Mini computers are originated in 1960s.
- Small mainframes that perform limited tasks.
- Less expensive than mainframe computer.
- Mini computers are Lower mainframe in the terms of processing capabilities.
- Capable of supporting 10 to 100 users simultaneously.
- In 1970s it contains 8 bit or 12 bit processor.
- Gradually the architecture requirement is grown and 16 and 32 bit.
- Minicomputers are invented which are known as supermini computers.
- Ex: IBM AS400

Mainframe Computer:

- A very powerful computer which capable of supporting thousands of user simultaneously.
- It contains powerful data processing system.
- It is capable to run multiple operating systems.
- It is capable to process 100 million instructions per second.
- Mainframes are very large & expensive computers with having larger internal storage capacity & high processing speed.
- Mainframes are used in the organization that need to process large number of transaction online & required a computer system having massive storage & processing capabilities.
- Mainly used to handle bulk of data & information for processing.
- Mainframe system is housed in a central location with several user terminal connected to it.
- Much bigger in size & needs a large rooms with closely humidity & temperature.
- IBM & DEC are major vendors of mainframes.
- Ex : MEDHA, SPERRY, IBM, DEC, HP, HCL

Super Computer:

- Most powerful & most expensive computer.
- Used for complex scientific application that requires huge processing power.
- Used multiprocessor technology to perform the calculation very speedy.
- They are special purpose computers that are designed to perform some specific task.

- The cost of the super computer is depended on its processing capabilities & configuration.
- The speed of modern computer is measured in gigaflops, teraflops and petaflops.
  - Gigaflops= 10^9 arithmetic operation per second.
  - Teraflops=10^{12} arithmetic operation per second.
  - Petaflops=10^{15} arithmetic operation per second.
- Ex: PARAM , EKA, BLUE GENE/P

6. EXPLAIN THE GENERATION OF THE COMPUTERS.

In Computer language, "Generation" is a set of Technology. It provides a framework for the growth of the computer technology. There are totally Five Computer Generations till today. Discussed as following.

First Generation:
- Duration: 1942-1955
- Technology: vacuum tube
  - Used as a calculating device.
  - Performed calculations in milliseconds.
  - To bulky in size & complex design.
  - Required large room to place it.
  - Generates too much heat & burnt.
  - Required continuously hardware maintenance.
  - Generates much heat so must air-conditioner rooms are required.
  - Commercial production is difficult & costly.
  - Difficult to configure.
  - Limited commercial use.
  - ENIAC, EDVAC, EDSAC are example of 1st generation computer.

Second Generation:
- Duration: 1955-1964
- Technology: transistor
  - 10 times Smaller in size than 1st generation system.
  - Less heat than 1st generation computers.
  - Consumed less power than 1st generation system.
  - Computers were done calculations in microseconds.
  - Air-conditioner is also required.
  - Easy to configure than 1st generation computers.

- o More reliable in information.
- o Wider commercial use.
- o Large & fast primary/secondary storage than 1st generation computers.

Third Generation:
- **Duration:**   1965-1975
- **Technology:**   IC chip
  - o Smaller in size than 1st & 2nd generation computers.
  - o Perform more fast calculations than 2nd generation systems.
  - o Large & fast primary/secondary storage than 2nd generation computers.
  - o Air –conditioner is required.
  - o Widely used for commercial applications.
  - o General purpose computers.
  - o High level languages like COBOL & FORTAN are allowed to write programs.
  - o Generate less heat & consumed less power than 2nd generation computer.

Fourth Generation:
- **Duration:**   1975-1989
- **Technology:**   Microprocessor chip
  - o Based on LSI & VLSI microprocessor chip.
  - o Smaller in size.
  - o Much faster than previous generations.
  - o Minimum hardware maintenance is required.
  - o Very reliable as computer to previous generation computers.
  - o Totally general purpose computer.
  - o Easy to configure.
  - o Possible to use network concept to connect the computer together.
  - o NO requirement of air-conditioners.
  - o Cheapest in price.

Fifth Generation:
- **Duration:**   1989 to Present
- **Technology:**   ULSI microprocessor chip
  - o Much smaller & handy.
  - o Based on the ULSI chip which contains 100 million electronic components.
  - o The speed of the operations is increased.
  - o Consumed less power.
  - o Air-conditioner is not required.
  - o More user friendly interface with multi-media features.
  - o High level languages are allowed to write programs.
  - o Larger & faster primary/secondary storage than previous generations.

o Notebook computers are the example of 5th generation computers.

7. EXPLAIN THE BLOCK DIAGRAM OF COMPUTER OR EXPLAIN THE SIMPLE MODEL COMPUTER.

A simple computer system comprises the basic components like Input Devices, CPU (Central Processing Unit) and Output Devices as under:

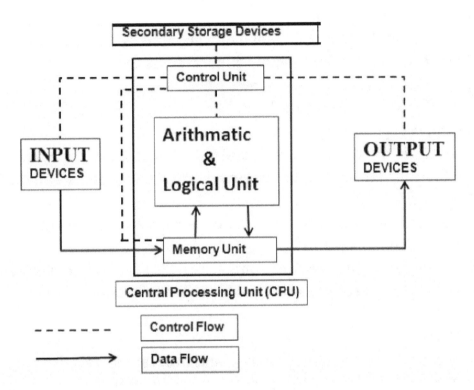

- **Input Devices:**
    - The devices which are used to entered data in the computer systems are known as input devices.
    - Keyboard, mouse, scanner, mike, light pen etc are example of input devices.

FUNCTION OF INPUT DEVICES
    - Accept the data from the outside worlds.
    - Convert that data into computer coded information.
    - Supply this data to CPU for further processing.

- **Output Devices:**
    - The devices which display the result generated by the computer are known as output devices.
    - Monitor, printer, plotter, speaker etc are the example of output devices.

FUNCTIONS OF OUTPUT DEVICES
    - Accept the result form the CPU.
    - Convert that result into human readable form.

o Display the result on the output device.

- **Memory Unit:**
  - o The data & instruction have to store inside the computer before the actual processing start.
  - o Same way the result of the computer must be stored before passed to the output devices. This tasks performed by memory unit.

  ## FUNCTIONS OF MEMORY UNIT
  - o Store data & instruction received from input devices.
  - o Store the intermediate results generated by CPU.
  - o Store the final result generated by CPU.

- **Arithmetical & Logical Unit:**
  - o The ALU is the place where actual data & instruction are processed.
  - o All the calculations are performed & all comparisons are made in ALU.
  - o Performs all arithmetical & logical operations.
  - o An arithmetic operation contains basic operations like addition, subtraction, multiplication, division.
  - o Logical operations contains comparison such as less than, greater than, less than equal to, greater than equal to, equal to, not equal to.

- **Control Unit:**
  - o It controls the movement of data and program instructions into and out of the CPU, and to control the operations of the ALU.
  - o In sort, its main function is to manage all the activities within the computer system.
  - o Controls the internal parts as well as the external parts related with the computer.

- **CPU:**
  - o The Unit where all the processing is done is called as Central Processing Unit.
  - o It contains many other units under it.
  - o Main of them are:- Control Unit And ALU (Arithmetic & Logic Unit)

UNIT: 2 INPUT DEVICES

1. WHAT IS INPUT DEVICES?

- The Input devices are the devices which are used to enter the data in the computer system.
- Keyboard, mouse, scanner, microphone are the example of input devices.

FUNCTIONS OF INPUT DEVICES:

- o Accept the data from the outside worlds.
- o Convert that data into computer coded information.
- o Supply this data to Central Processing Unit for further processing.

CLASIFICATION OF INPUT DEVICES:

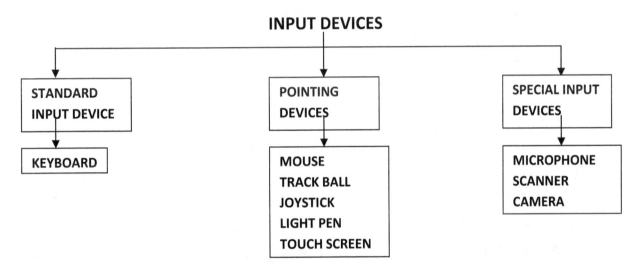

2. EXPLAIN STANDARD INPUT DEVICE: KEYBOARD.

- Keyboard is most commonly used input device.
- It is similar like a type writer which is used to enter data in the computer.
- It contains sets of keys such as alphabets, number & special signs.
- There are two types of keyboard.
    - o General purpose keyboard
    - o Special purpose keyboard

GENERAL PURPOSE KEYBOARD:

- Standard keyboard which are used in personal computers.
- It contains enough keys which are used in all types of applications so they are known as general purpose keyboard.
- Most popular general purpose keyboard contains 101 keys.
- The general purpose keyboard are divided into following parts:

ALPHANUMERAIC KEYPAD

- The centred part of the keyboard is known as alphanumeric keypad.
- It contains alphabets, numbers & special signs such as *,!, @, #, $, %,* etc.

NUMERAIC KEYPAD

- The right most part of the keyboard is known as numeric keypad.
- It contains 0 to 9 numbers & mathematical signs such as +, *, -, /.
- Mainly used for fast data entry in mathematical applications.

ARROW KEYS

- Set of four keys up, down, left & right.
- Used to move the cursor at left & right or up and down on the screen.
- They are referred as "cursor-control" or "cursor-movement" keys.

FUNCTION KEYS

- The first line of the keyboard contains a Set of 12 keys with name f1 to f2 are known as function keys.
- Used to generate short-cuts in different software package.

SPECIAL KEYS

- There are lots of keys that are used for some specific task describes follows:
- TAB: used for gives multiple spaces or move the cursor to next defined position.
- ENTER: used for generate the output of any command.
- SPACE: used to make one blank space between two words.
- BACKSPACE: used to remove the left-most character at cursor position.
- DELETE: used to remove the right-most character at cursor position.
- HOME: moves the cursor at the beginning of the line.
- END: moves cursor at the end of the line.
- PAGE UP: moves or scroll the screen up or previous page of the current page.
- PAGE DOWN: moves the screen to the next page from the currently displayed page.
- PRINT SCREEN: used to print what is currently displayed on the screen.
- INSERT: used to enter text between two characters.

- **ESC:** used to negate current command or terminate the execution of the program.
- **ALT:** used to expand the functionality of keyboard. Basically used to generate shortcuts in different application.
- **CTRL:** used to expand the functionality of keyboard. Basically used to generate shortcuts in different application.
- **NUMLOCK:** used to on or off the numeric keypad.
- **CAPSLOCK:** used to type the all inputted text capitally.

SPECIAL PURPOSE KEYBOARD

- Special purpose keyboard is used for special purpose applications which required faster data entry and rapid interaction with the computer system.
- For example ATM used in banks used special purpose keyboard which contains a few keys.

3. EXPLAIN POINTING DEVICES.

1. MOUSE

- Mouse is Small hand-hold device Input device which is generally used for drawing purpose.
- It's a Pointing device.
- It contains two or three buttons
- Left button is used to point out or select any item by clicking.
- Right to generate context menu.
- When user moves mouse across flat surface, the graphic cursor moves on screen.
- Graphic cursor contains verity of symbols such as arrow, wrist, pointing finger etc.
- Depending on application text & graphic cursors are changed.
- The following 5 techniques are used to carry out various operations:
- POINT:
  - To move the mouse on top of icon
- C LICK:
  - To press & release the left button of mouse at once.
  - Used to open any currently selected icon, menu.
- DOUBLE CLICK:
  - To press & release the left button of mouse twice.
  - Used to open any application or program.

- **SIMULTANEOUS-CLICK:**
  - Press & release left & right button to gather.
  - Used in some software package to added some functionality.
- **DRAG:**
  - Press the left button down & moved the mouse on screen.
  - Used to move the graphics on screen.
- Many types of mouse are available such as mechanical mouse, optical mouse, serial mouse, wireless mouse which are used for different purpose.

2. TRACK BALL

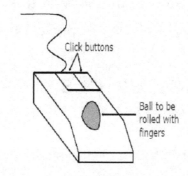

Click buttons

Ball to be rolled with fingers

Commonly used in laptop (notebook) computers

- Trackball is a pointing device which is similar to a mouse.
- A ball is placed on the track ball device which is used to move the graphic cursor on the screen.
- It also contains buttons which are used to select a particular item on the screen.
- To move the graphic cursor on screen, the ball is rolled with the fingers or thumb.
- It needs not to move the whole device to move the cursor so it is often attached with some keyboards.
- Track balls come in various shapes with same functionality.
- Commonly three shapes are used: ABALL, A SQUARE, and A SQUARE.
- In case of ball we need to move it with the help of finger.
- In case of button pushed with finger in desired direction of the cursor movement.
- In case of button press finger to up or down & left or right to move cursor.
  <u>Advantages of track ball</u>
  - Takes less desk space.

- Takes less arm movements than mouse.
- Doesn't require any mouse pad & large area to move the mouse.
- Less strain on the wrist.
- Finger trip control which may offer more accuracy than mouse.

3. JOYSTICK

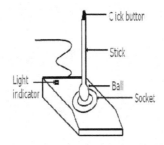

Commonly used for video games, flight simulators, training simulators, and for controlling industrial robots

- Joystick is a pointing device which is works on the same principle of track ball.
- It contains a stick which is placed on the spherical ball.
- The stick is used to move the cursor at desired position left or right or backward or forward.
- It also contain button that is clicked to make selection of currently pointed item.
- A joystick is similar to a mouse, except that with a mouse the cursor stops moving as soon as you stop moving the mouse.
- With a joystick, the pointer continues moving in the direction the joystick is pointing.
- To stop the pointer, you must return the joystick to its upright position.
- Some of the systems using joysticks are
  o Aircrafts, UAVs for flight control
  o Motorized Wheelchairs as input device
  o Microscopes
  o Submarines
  o Security Systems
  o Video Games
- Joysticks are widely used for video games
- Advantages of joystick
- It is very easy to learn to use.

- Very simple design so they can be inexpensive.
- It has a big analogue stick in the middle so it's easier to control.

4. LIGHT PEN

- Light pen is a pointing device which is used to draw directly draw on the screen.
- It is called light pen because it is similar to a pen & senses light.
- It's an input device in the form of light-sensitive stick used in conjunction with a CRT display.
- The light pen allows the user to point out or draw any object on the screen.
- The user brings the pen to the desired point on screen and presses the pen button to make contact.
- It has a switch on its top which allows the user to make contact with screen.
- It is useful for drawing or graphics in the program such as CAD (computer aided design).
- An engineer, architect or fashion designer can draw directly on screen.
- Used in application such as gaming, graphic arts, healthcare applications etc.
- Light pen cannot scratch or damage a screen.

Advantages of light pen;
  - Less expensive than touch screen.
  - give the user the full range of mouse capabilities, without the use of a pad or any horizontal surface
  - Cannot scratch or damage screen.
  - Works on any size screen.

5. TOUCH SCREEN

- Touch screen is a pointing device.
- It is most simple & easiest to learn of all input devices.

- It allows the user to choose from available options by simply touching with their figure to the desired icon or menu item displayed on the computer screen.
- A touch screen is an electronic visual display that can detect the presence and location of a touch within the display area.
- The term generally refers to touching the display of the device with a finger or hand.
- Touch screens are common in devices such as computers, tablet computers & Smartphone.
- The touch screen has two main attributes::
  - First, it enables one to interact directly with what is displayed.
  - Secondly, it lets one do so without requiring any intermediate device that would need to be held in the hand
- It's a very easy to operate device which users can use the system without any formal training.
- Uses optical sensors that detect the touch of the finger on screen.
- Sensors communicate the position of touch to the computer which interprets the input made by the users.
- It contains pressure sensitive monitors which are placed inside the base of computer screen.
- Pressure sensitive monitors contain sensors to measure the monitor's weight at many points.
- When user touches the screen, the changes on weights & forces transferred down to sensor which allows the device to detect the location of the touch.
- This type of monitors required little pressure to transmit the desired input.
- Touch screen are commonly used in following places.
  - An airport or railway station.
  - Large departmental stores.
  - In large museums or zoos to guide visitors to the locations of various attractions.
  - Self service check out
  - In ATM machines
  - In I-phones or PDA's
  - Computer based training
- Any type of touch screen contains Three main components:

A touch screen sensor panel:

- Which sits above the display & generate appropriate voltage according to where precisely it is touched?

A touch screen controller:
- Processes the signal received from the sensor & translates this touch event data & passed to pc's processor via serial or USB interface.

A soft ware driver:
- Provides an interface to the pc's operating system & which translates the touch event data into mouse event.

6. DIGITIZER

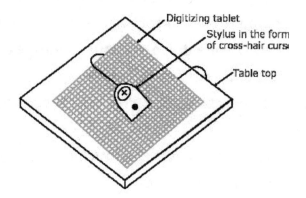

- An input device.
- Used for converting pictures, map & drawing into digital form.
- Allows one to hand-draw images and graphics, similar to the way one draws images with a pencil and paper.
- Also be used to capture data or handwritten signatures.
- The device consists of a flat surface upon which the user may "draw" an image using an attached stylus, a pen-like drawing tool.
- These devices are usually connected via a Serial port.
- Placed on the desk n connected with the computer.
- Digitizer consists of graphic tablets which are associated with a stylus.
- The stylus is like a pen with a button.
- Stylus connected with a tablet and can press down at a point on the tablet to input (x, y) co-ordinates of point.
- It contains hundreds of copper wires forming a grid that receives electric pulsed.
- When stylus moves on tables the cursor on screen moves simultaneously.
- Allows the user to draw sketches directly.
- Commonly used in CAD by architects & engineers.

- Used in GIS (geographical information system) for digitizing maps.

7. MICROPHONE

- It's an input device.
- Used to stores the voice data into the computer system.
- Microphones are a type of *transducer* - a device which converts energy from one form to another.
- Microphones convert sound waves into electrical energy.
- Different types of microphone have different ways of converting energy.

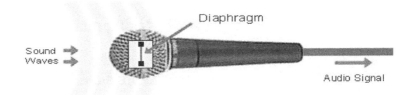

- All the microphones share one common thing: The diaphragm.
- Thin piece of material (such as paper, plastic or aluminium) which vibrates when it is struck by sound waves.
- When the diaphragm vibrates, it causes other components in the microphone to vibrate.
- These vibrations are converted into an electrical current which becomes the audio signal.
- The microphones are divided in mainly two types

The type of conversion technology they use
- o This refers to the technical method the mike uses to convert sound into electricity.
- o The most common technologies are dynamic, condenser, ribbon and crystal.

The type of application they are designed for
- o Some mikes are designed for general use and others are much specialised purpose.

8. WEB CAMERA

- It's an input device.
- Used to feeds the image to a computer or computer network often via USB or Wi-Fi.

- Web camera is a hardware camera connected to a computer that allows everyone to connect to internet to view either pictures or motion video.
- Most Web cameras are embedded to display with laptop computer or connected with USB or Wi-Fi with a computer.
- Simple web cam. Consists a digital camera attached to your computer typically through USB.
- The camera part of web camera is just a digital camera.
- Web camera comes with software which preset interval & transfer it to another location of viewing.
- Web camera system allows you to using video also for that you have web camera with high frame rate.
- Web camera is a digital camera which taking picture over & over & again one after another.
- These images are stored image into the physical memory of camera in built in.
- After capture image & stored in memory it reduced the amount of data need to transmit.
- Web camera software takes image & converts data in jpeg (compressing format).

9. EXPLAIN SCANNER & ITS TYPES.

- Scanners are input devices.
- They are capable of entering information directly into the computer.
- The main advantage of direct entry of information is that users do not have to key the information.
- And another advantage is that through Scanners you can input Graphical Data into the computer. This
- Provides faster and more accurate data entry. Important types of scanners

Image scanner:

- It's an input device, which translates paper documents into an electronic format which can b stored in a computer.
- The input document may be typed text, pictures, graphics or even handwritten material.
- There are two types of image scanner:

Flatbed scanner

- It's like a zerox machine which consist of box having a glass plate on its top and a lid to covers the glass plate.
- The document placed inside the glass plate & light source is situated blow glass plate which moves horizontally from left to write & scanning document line by line.

Handheld scanner

- It contains a set of light emitting diodes encased in small case which can be conveniently held in hand.
- To scan a document the scanner is slowly dragged on the document.
- The scanner has to be dragged carefully & steadily otherwise the document cannot scan properly.
- Used when higher accuracy is not required.

10. EXPLAIN THE OPTICAL SCANNERS

OMR (OPTICAL MARK READER)

- OMR is a device that is capable of recognised pre-specified type of mark made by pencil or pen.
- The Optical Mark Reader is a device which can detect the presence or absence of a mark on a paper.
- The OMR recognise the marks by focusing a light on the paper being scanned & detect the reflected light pattern from mark.
- The present mark is detected due to intensity of light being reflected from the mark.
- Pencil marks made with soft lead pencil reflect the light which allowing the OMR to determine which response are mark.
- OMR is used in reading answers sheets, questionnaires.

ADVANTAGES

- Speedy and accurate to generate result.
- Cheap in cost.

DISADVANTAGE

- Cannot able to read characters.
- Erasing or cancellation is not possible.
- Good quality expensive paper is required.

OCR (OPTICAL CHARACTER READER) DEVICE

- OCR capable of recognizing alphabets & numbers printed on paper.
- It can also capable of recognise shape & identify character directly from source document.
- It is always used with character recognized software.
- It converts bitmap images of character to equivalent ASCII code.
- First it create bitmap image of document & OCR software translate into ASCII code which computer interprets letter, symbol or number.
- The type of document must be type using OCR fonts.
- The software design to recognised the standard OCR-A(American standard) & OCR-B(European standard)

ADVANTAGES

- Speedy entered data.
- Accept wide range of font using ordinary mark.

DISADVANTAGE

- Expensive
- Scanned properly only if the characters are standard size.
- Dusty paper cant scanned properly.

MICR (MAGNETIC INK CHARACTER RECOGNITION)

- MICR systems use special ink which can be magnetized, to print characters that can then be read and decoded by special magnetic devices.
- The common E13B font is used to write these special kinds of cheques.
- E13B font contains 0-9 numbers & 4 symbols.
- Detection of characters is a two step process.
- First MICR Reader-Sorter reads the data on cheques & sorts the cheques for distribution for further processing.
- The reading station is used to sense and identify the magnetic characters as they pass through.
- Magnetized characters are read by the head. E.g. MICR is used in Banks to cheques the MICR systems use special ink which can be magnetized, to print characters cheques.

ADVANTAGES

- Speedy data entry.
- Accurate output.
- Folded or roughly handled cheques are also scanned with same accuracy.
  DISADVANTAGE
- MICR software is required.
- Limited fonts are used so used in banking industries only.

BCR (BAR CODE READER) DEVICE

- Data can be coded in the form of small lines which are known as Bar Codes.
- Bar codes represent the alphanumeric data by combination of vertical lines which contains different width & spacing between them.
- Bar Code Reader is a device which are used to recognized bar code data.
- It scanned the barcode image & converted into alphanumeric value & fed to computer.
- It uses laser-beam technology. Laser stroke across the pattern of bar which sensed by light sensitive decoder & their reflection of light pattern are converted into electrical pulse which converted it into alphanumeric value.
- Various barcodes are available for different use.
- Most common is UPC (UNIVERSAL PRODUCT CODE).

It contain 10 digit first 5 identify the manufacturer name & remaining identify a specific product.

UNIT: 3 OUTPUT DEVICES

1. WHAT IS OUTPUT DEVICE.

- The output devices are the devices which are used to display the result generated by the computer system.
- Monitor, printer, plotter, speaker are the example of output devices.

FUNCTIONS OF INPUT DEVICES:

- Accept the result from the CPU.
- Convert that result into human readable form.
- Supply this result to output device.

2. EXPLAIN THE VISUAL DISPLAY UNIT

OR

EXPLAIN CRT (CATHOD RAY TUBE) MONITER.

- The monitor is the common output device mostly used It is a softcopy output device.
- It can be thought of as a high resolution TV set.
- The monitor can also determine if the display will be colour, black and white, or include graphical objects (pictures).
- Two types of monitors are used.
    - CRT monitors.
    - Non CRT monitors.
- Most computer monitors are based on Cathode Ray Tube (CRT) technology.
- The basic operation of these tubes is similar to that in television sets.

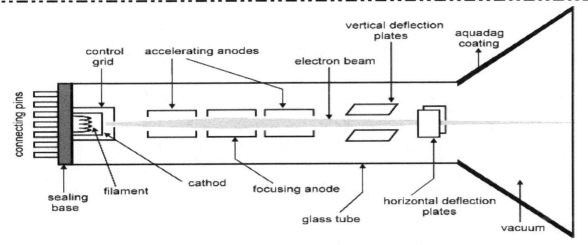

- In CRT display CRT is a specialised vacuum tube in which images are produced when electron beam strikes a phosphor surface.
- CRT monitor contains cathode, control grid, acceleration anode, deflection plates & phosphor coated screen.
- Cathode: the cathode is heated by filament and produced high speed & large amount of electrons.
- Control Grid: used to control the brightness of the screen. It controls the number of electrons.
- Accelerating anodes: they are with focusing lens are applied with positive electrons.
- Horizontal deflection plate: moves electron side by side.
- Vertical deflection: moves electrons up & down.
- Screen: contains millions of tiny red, green, blue phosphor dot that glow when struck by electron beam that travels across screen to create a visible image.

ADVANTAGES OF CRT DISPLAY

- Produce more colours.
- Price is lower than LCD & Plasma.
- High contrast ratio.
- Can easily increase brightness of monitor by reflecting the light.

DISADVANTAGES OF CRT DISPLAY

- High power consumed.
- Heavy to pick up and carry.
- Large space required.

3. EXPLAIN THE NON CRT DISPLAY.

LCD (Liquid Crystal Display)

- In LCD, a liquid crystalline material is sandwiched between two glass or a plastic plates.

- The front plate is transparent and the back plate is reflective.
- There is a coating of thin film on the front plate.
- The coating is transparent and conductive. Its sections (segments) are in the shape of desired characters.
- LCDs do not emit their own light. Therefore, a light source is to be used.
- LCDs simply change the reflection of available light. Today, most LCDs used are of the type that produces dark images on a silver background.

Advantages:

- Light weight as compare to CRT.
- Perfectly flat screen.
- Consumed low electricity power.
- Able to generate higher brightness in images.

Disadvantages:

- Fixed resolution that cannot be changed.
- Expensive than CRT display.
- Limited viewing angle.
- Short life.

PDP (Plasma Displays Panel)

- In Plasma Displays, ionized gas is sandwiched between two glass plates.
- A number of parallel wires run horizontally as well as vertically.
- A small amount of current is passed through one horizontal and one vertical wire to cause the gas to glow at a spot at the intersection of the wires.
- The IBM 581 display employs 960 horizontal and 768 vertical pixel as compared to IBM-PC colour graphic adapter which is provided with 320 X 200 pixels in medium resolution and 640 X 200 in high resolution.

Advantages:

- Large viewing angle.
- Thinner in width.
- Free standing or can be easily mounted on wall.
- Clear image, brighter viewing angle, better colour quality & high contrast ratio.

Disadvantages:

- The plasma displays screens are costly.
- These are available on the selected models of portable computers.
- More electricity than LCD.

- As your plasma get older the brightness get dimmer.

4. WHAT IS PRINTER? EXPLAIN THE TYPES OF PRINTER.

Printer

- The printer is a most commonly used output device.
- It is used to producing the hard copy output.
- It prints characters, symbols & graphics on the paper.
- Printer can be categorised according to the technology used in printer, speed, and approach of printing, colours, language & the quality of printing.
- Mainly printer can be classified in two types:
  - Impact printer
  - Non impact printer

IMPACT PRINTER:

- It works on the same mechanism of type-writer.
- It forms a character or image by striking mechanism such as hammer or wheel against to ink ribbon, leaving an image on paper.
- It is oldest technology and still is in used.
- It can capable to print single character or line at the same time.
- Commonly types of impact printers are dot matrix, daisy wheel, chain, drum printer.

CHARACTERISTICS OF IMPACT PRINTER:

  - Physical contact with paper to produce output.
  - Low cost
  - Very noisy
  - Very slow in printing
  - Low quality print out
  - Stand with dusty or extreme environment

NON IMPACT PRINTER:

- Non impact printer forms characters & images on paper without actually striking the paper.
- Paper & print head come in contact & hence the text or image is formed.
- Ink jet & laser printer are example of non impact printer.

CHARACTERISTICS OF NON IMPACT PRINTER

  - Faster than impact printer.

- o Ability to change type face automatically.
- o High quality output.
- o Support transparency.
- o More expensive than impact printer.
- o Less maintenance than impact printer.

5. <u>EXPLAIN IMPACT PRINTERS.</u>

<u>Dot matrix printer:</u>

- Character printer.
- Capable to print single character at the same time.
- Forms characters & images as a pattern of dots.
- Contains a print head which moves horizontally across paper.
- Uses 5 × 7 matrix to form a character.
- Print by hammering the pins on inked ribbon to leave ink impressions on the paper.
- <u>Able to print 30 to 600 characters per second</u>.
- <u>ADVANTAGES:</u>
  - o Low cost & easily available.
  - o Cheap in cost.
  - o Can make carbon copy of print out.
  - o Low maintenance cost.
  - o Work with any type of environment.
- <u>DISADVANTAGES:</u>
  - o Slow in speed.
  - o Very noisy.
  - o Cannot work perfectly in graphics.

<u>DAISY WHEEL PRINTER:</u>

- Character printer.
- Able to print a single character at the same time.
- Contain a metal wheel on which the characters & numbers are raised on the each petal.
- The wheel is rotated very fast when the desired characters arrives at correct position a print hammer strike to produce output.
- Different type of font face can be used by replacing the daisy wheel.
- Able to print bold letter by striking on specific characters twice or thrice.

- Capable to print 10 to 50 characters per second.
- **ADVANTAGES:**
  - Low cost.
  - Can make carbon copy of print out.
  - Low maintenance cost.
  - Printing quality is similar to a type writer.
  - Able to print bold characters.
  - Allows using different font-face in same document.
- **DISADVANTAGES:**
  - Very slow in speed.
  - Very noisy.
  - Cannot print graphics.

DRUM PRINTER:

- It's a line printer.
- Able to print a line at the same time.
- Consist of a solid cylindrical drum with characters embossed on it in circular band.
- Each band consists of character set which contains 96 characters.
- Drum rotates fastly when desired characters arrives an appropriate hammer stike on ribbon & character is print on paper.
- Capable to print 300 to 2000 lines per minute.
- **ADVANTAGES:**
  - Low cost than non impact printer.
  - Can make carbon copy of print out.
  - Low maintenance cost.
  - Faster than other impact printer.
  - Printing quality is similar to a type writer.
- **DISADVANTAGES:**
  - Very slow in speed.
  - Very noisy.
  - Large & heavy.
  - Cannot print graphics.
  - Only prints predefined set of characters.

CHANIN PRINTER:

- It's a line printer.

- Able to print a line at the same time.
- Consist of a metallic chain on which all characters of character set are embossed.
- Character set contains 48, 64 or 96 characters.
- Characters are embossed several times.
- Chain rotates at high speed when the desired characters in correct position the hammer strikes & the characters are print on paper.
- Capable to print 400 to 2500 lines per minutes.
- ADVANTAGES:
    - Low cost than non impact printer.
    - Can make carbon copy of print out.
    - Chain can be easily changed.
    - Allowed to print different type font.
    - Printing quality is similar to a type writer.
- DISADVANTAGES:
    - Slower than non impact printer.
    - Very noisy.
    - Large & heavy.
    - Cannot print graphics.
    - Only prints predefined set of characters.

7. EXPALAIN NON-IMPACT PRINTERS.

INK-JET PRINTER:

- It's non-impact printer.
- It's a character printer.
- Forms characters and all kinds of images by spraying drops of ink on to the paper.
- Print head contains 64 tiny nozzles.
- To print a character the printer the printer selectively heats the appropriate set of nozzle as the print head moves horizontally.
- Inkjet printer can either colour or monochrome.
- Capable to print 30 to 400 characters per minutes.
- ADVANTAGES:
    - High quality output.
    - Silent during the operation.
    - Able to print graphics.
    - Able to print any characters & graphics.

- o Able to generate colour & monochrome output.
- **DISADVANTAGES:**
  - o Slower than dot matrix printer.
  - o Cannot make carbon copy of print out.
  - o Expensive than impact printer.

LASER PRINTER:

- It's non-impact printer.
- It's a page printer.
- Three main components laser beam, a multi-sided mirror, a photoconductive drum & toner.
- To print page laser beam is focused on drum by spinning multisided mirror.
- Drum is electric charged.
- Toner which is composed of oppositely charged ink particles, stick to the drum.
- Then toner focused on the paper with heat & pressure to generate output.
- Low speed laser printer can print 4 to 12 page per minute while high speed laser printer Capable to print 500 to 1000 pages per minutes.
- **ADVANTAGES:**
  - o High quality output.
  - o Very faster in speed.
  - o Silent during the operation.
  - o Able to print graphics.
  - o Able to print any characters & graphics.
  - o Able to generate colour & monochrome output.
- **DISADVANTAGES:**
  - o Very expensive.
  - o Cannot make carbon copy of print out.

8. WRITE DOWN THE DIFFERENCE BETWEEN IMPACT & NON-IMPACT PRINTER.

Impact printer	Non impact printer
Printing character by striking hammer against ink ribbon to produce output	Printing characters or graphics by spraying ink on paper.
Slow in speed	Faster than impact printer
Work with any environment	Can't work with all environment
Less expensive than non impact printer	More expensive than impact printer

Noisy during printing	Silent during printing
Able to produced carbon copy output	Cant able to produced carbon copy output
e.g.: daisy wheel, drum, chain, dot matrix	e.g.: inkjet, laser

9. WHAT IS PLOTTER? EXPLAIN ITS TYPE.

Plotter:

- Plotter is an output device which is capable to producing hardcopy output of graphics.
- Used to producing wide format printing.
- It is an ideal output device for architects, engineers, city planners and other who need to generate hardcopy output of widely varying in sizes.
- Woks on the same mechanism of human holding pen & moving on paper.
- Contains multiple pens & pencil which can be easily changed out in order to create drawing of different colours.
- Normally generate output very slowly.
- Mainly two types of plotters are used:
  - Drum plotter
  - Flatbed

Drum plotter:

- In the case design has to be made is placed over a drum.
- It consist one or more than penholders which are mounted to the drum surface.
- The drum plotter both the paper and the pen move.
- The paper is contained on two rollers and passes over a drum.
- The pen is driven along fixed arm set across the length of the drum.
- It is especially useful for plotting continuous line graph.
- The accuracy of the drum type depends on the paper transport mechanism, which in turn is dependent on the width of the paper and it can also produce larger drawings.

Flatbed Plotter

- The Flatbed Plotter is generally more expensive and can produce very detailed and accurate drawings.
- The paper is mounted on a stationary flatbed.

- The pen is mounted on a moveable arm.
- Colour drawing can be produced by some plotters through interchangeable pens.
- Able to draw output in small size as A4 size or can able to generate very large size can be up to 20ft by 50ft.
- Specially used in the design of cars, ships, aircrafts, buildings, highways etc.

9. WRITE A BRIEF NOTE ON SPEAKER.

- The speaker is output device which is connected to computer's soundcard.
- The speaker output the sound generated by the sound card.
- Audio data is generated by computer is send to audio card which is located inside extension slot.
- It can translate data into audio signal which are sending to speaker.
- The speaker can able to produced series of different tones.

UNIT: 4 INTERNAL/EXTERNAL PARTS WITH COMPUTER CABINATE

1. EXPLAIN TYPES OF PROCESSORS.
DUAL CORE

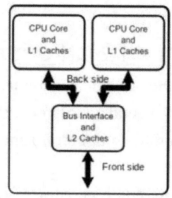

- Dual-core refers to a CPU that includes two complete execution cores per physical processor.
- It has combined two processors and their caches and cache controllers onto a single integrated circuit (silicon chip)
- Multi-core is similar to dual-core in that it is an expansion to the dual-core technology which allows for more than two separate processors.
- Dual-core refers to a CPU that includes two complete execution cores per physical processor.
- It combines two processors and their caches and cache controllers onto a single integrated circuit (silicon chip).
- It is basically two processors, in most cases, residing reside side-by-side on the same die.
- Dual-core processors are well-suited for multitasking environments because there are two complete execution cores instead of one.
- Each with an independent interface to the front side bus.
- Since each core has its own cache, the operating system has sufficient resources to handle most compute intensive tasks in parallel.

ADVANTAGES:
- Performance is faster than single-core processors.
- Able to divide information for processing by multiple units.
- Core processor uses slightly less power than two coupled single-core processors

- Multi-core chips also allow higher performance at lower energy.

CORE 2 DUO

- Core 2 Duo is the name given by Intel to its second batch of dual core processors.
- Desktop PCs with the Intel® Core™2 processor family deliver faster performance, greater energy efficiency, and more responsive multitasking.
- Intel's dual core processors were simply 2 Pentium 3 processors that were fabricated in a single chip.
- As they refined their product more, they decided to differentiate their second set of processors from the Core Duo and decided to call it Core 2 Duo.
- The difference between dual core processors and the Core 2 Duo processors is just in the semantics as Core 2 Duo is simply a name given to a more recent family of dual core processors.
- If we translate this to the single core processors, we can say that Core Duo is Pentium 1 while Core 2 Duo is Pentium 2. But all these are still single core processors.
- We can therefore say that Core 2 Duo is simply a subset of all the dual core processors that are out in the market today.

Features and benefits

- With an Intel® Core™2 Duo processor you will get performance-rich technologies,
- Intel® multi-core processing provides greater multitasking performance by combining two independent processor cores in one physical package.
- Execution improves execution time and energy efficiency with more instructions per clock cycle.
- Power Capability enables smarter, more energy-efficient performance.
- Intel® Smart Memory Access improves system performance by optimizing the use of the available data bandwidth
- Intel® Advanced Smart Cache enables higher performance and more efficient cache subsystem by optimizing for multi-core processors.

2. EXPLAIN PRIMORY STORAGE DEVICE.

- It's a temporary storage.
- It consists of some chips.
- The data & instruction are resided in this memory when the CPU executing programs.
- This memory can capable to store & retrieved data very quickly.
- Primary memory is only the memory that is directly access to the CPU.

RAM

- The complete name of RAM is random access memory which is also known as Primary memory.
- It is called read/write memory because data can be read as well as write in RAM.
- It is called random access because you can directly access any data from RAM if you know row & column cell.
- The RAM chip is fixed on the mother board & the mother board is designed in such a way that its memory capacity can be enhanced by adding more RAM chip.
- RAM is a VOLETILE memory.
- RAM chips are of two types:

DRAM:

- Dynamic Random Access Memory is a volatile memory that allows fast access to data and is ideal for use as the primary store of computer systems.
- However, the information is stored as electrical charges and the charges need to be constantly refreshed in order for the data to be maintained.

SRAM:

- Static Random Access Memory is also a volatile memory.
- Once data is written into the chip, it is maintained as long as power is supplied to it; it does not need refreshing.
- However, SRAM is slower than DRAM and it is also more expensive.

ROM

- The complete name of ROM is read only memory.
- The data stored permanently & can't be altered by the programmer.
- Data stored in RAM chip can be read & used but cannot be changed.
- This memory also known a field storage permanent storage or dead storage.
- It is basically used to store manufacturer programmed & user program.
- Most of the basic operations are carried out by electronic circuits which are known as micro programs.
- These programs are stored in ROM. For ex. System Boot Loader.

ROM

- The complete name of ROM is read only memory.
- The data stored permanently & can't be altered by the programmer.
- Data stored in RAM chip can be read & used but cannot be changed.

PROM

- Programmable Read Only Memory is a non-volatile memory which allows the user to program the chip with a PROM writer.

- The chip can be programmed once, thereafter, it cannot be altered.

EPROM & EEPROM

- Erasable Programmable Read Only Memory and Electrically Erasable Programmable Read Only Memory chips can be electrically programmed.
- Unlike ROM and PROM chips, EPROM chips can be erased and reprogrammed.

3. EXPLAIN FOLLOING PORTS

SERIAL PORT

- Known as asynchronous port or RS-232-C port.
- This type of port is sends & receives data using only two line.
- Therefore this type of port is ideal for connection to the phone circuits which uses 2 data lines.
- The communication process of data transfer is slower.
- Due to this reason it is not used for printer.
- It has high signal travelling capacity.

PARALLEL PORT

- Known as centronics or printer port.
- It's a type of socket found on personal computer for connecting various types of computer devices.
- Normally it is reserved for printer.
- They carry 8 bits at the same time so that communication becomes very faster.
- Due to the faster data communication capability it is used in input & output devices.
- The signal travel capacity is less than serial port.

USB PORT

- It's a new interface technology which are used to connect computer peripherals such as keyboard, mouse, scanner, joysticks, printer, web camera etc.
- USB operate at two speeds 1.5 mbps & 12 mbps.
- The speed is depending upon the devices which are attached with the port.
- For example the devices such as mouse, keyboard Use the law band while digital camera use high speed channel/
- Main advantage is that when devices are attached the appropriate drivers are loaded automatically.

PS/2 PORT

- Developed by IBM for connecting mouse or keyboard to PC.
- It supports the plug that contains 6 pins.
- Also called mouse port.

4. EXPLAIN FOLLOWING CABLES

Serial Cable

- Serial Cables are typically used for RS-232 communication.
- A serial cable is a cable that can be used to transfer information between two devices using serial communication.
- The form of connectors depends on the particular serial port used.
- The maximum working length of a cable varies depending on the characteristics of the transmitters and receivers.
- This cable has short transmission distance because of noise limiting the transmission of high numbers of bits per second when the cable is more than 15 meters long.
- It is cheap to purchase and is simple to join and connect.
- It is suitable for unbalanced data standards.
- Only one device can be connected to the cable.

Parallel Cable

- On many legacy peripherals, the parallel cable utilized both the 25 pin Sub-D connector and the 36 pin Centronics connector.
- This was a common printer interface and is still in service in great numbers.
- With the advent of "intelligent" laser and ink jet printers, the IEEE-1284 bi-directional printer cable was introduced.
- This parallel interface allows for bi-directional communication resulting in speeds up to 10 times faster than conventional cables.

USB Cable

- To Connecting a USB device to a computer is simple -- you find the USB connector on the back of your machine and plug the USB connector into it.
- If it's a new device, the operating system auto-detects it and asks for the driver disk.
- If the device has already been installed, the computer activates it and starts talking to it.
- USB devices can be connected and disconnected at any time.

5. SHORT NOTE: GRAPHIC CARDS.

- A graphics card is the component in your computer that handles generating the signals that are sent to the monitor or "graphics".
- It is responsible for generating all the text and pictures that are displayed on your screen.

- The images you see on your monitor are made of tiny dots called pixels.
- At most common resolution settings, a screen displays over a million pixels, and the computer has to decide what to do with everyone in order to create an image.
- To do this, it needs a translator -- something to take binary data from the CPU and turn it into a picture you can see.
- This task is performed by Graphic Card which is built into motherboard.
- A graphics card's job is complex, but its principles and components are easy to understand.
- The CPU, working in conjunction with software applications, sends information about the image to the graphics card.
- The graphics card decides how to use the pixels on the screen to create the image.
- It then sends that information to the monitor through a cable.
- To make a 3-D image, the graphics card first creates a wire frame out of straight lines. Then, it rasterizes the image.
- It also adds lighting, texture and colour.
- The graphics card accomplishes this task using four main components:
  - A motherboard connection for data and power
  - A processor to decide what to do with each pixel on the screen
  - Memory to hold information about each pixel and to temporarily store completed pictures
  - A monitor connection so you can see the final result

UNIT: 5 DATA STORAGE

1. WRITE A NOTE ON MAGNETIC TAPE

- Sequentially access storage device.
- Most popular storage medium for storage large data.
- Its plastic ribbon which is ½ or ¼ inch wide and 50 to 2400 feet long.
- It is coated with a magnetisable recording material.
- In a magnetic tape data are recorded serially.
- Information is recorded on the tape in the form of tiny invisible magnetized and non magnetized spots.
- The tape ribbon is itself stored in reels or small cassette.
- Whenever we stored new data on the tape that contains old data the old data are automatically erased and new data are recorded in the same area.
- In older tape contains 7 tracks and they used 6-bit BCD code format for data recording.
- Morden magnetic tape contains 9 tracks & used 8-bit EBCDIC code format for data recording.
- There are various types of magnetic tape are used. Most commonly are:
    - ½ inch tape reel
    - ½ inch tape cartridge
    - ¼ inch streamer tape
    - 4 mm digital audio tape

Advantages:

- Large or unlimited storage capacity.
- Low cost.
- Light weight and compact in size.
- Copying of data is easy and fast.
- Possible to erase older data n store new data.

Disadvantages:

- Cannot be accessed directly because it's a Sequential access device.
- Must be located in dust free environment otherwise it cause errors.
- Data are stored in coded form so cannot interpret or verify directly.

2. <u>WRITE A NOTE ON MAGNETIC TAPE</u>

- Directly access storage device.
- It's a thin circular plate that is made up with plastic material.
- Plate is coated both side with magnetic material such as iron oxide.
- Information is recorded on the tape in the form of tiny invisible magnetized and non magnetized spots.
- 8-bit EBCDIC code is used for data recording.
- Like magnetic tapes, magnetic disks are also erased & reuse.
- The disk is divided into number of circles called tracks.
- The tracks are further divided into sectors.
- A sector typically contains 512 bytes.

---

storage capacity of disk =number of recording surface * number of track per surface * number of sector per tracks * number of bytes per sectors

---

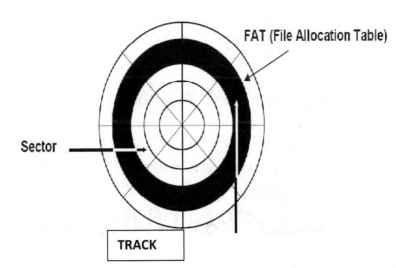

- Two common types of magnetic disks are used widely.
  - Floppy disks
  - Hard disks

3. <u>SHORT NOTE: FLOPPY DISK</u>

- Floppy disks were introduced by IBM in 1972.

- A floppy disk is a round, flat piece of flexible plastic which is coated with magnetic oxide.
- It is encased in square plastic cover that gives protection to the disk.
- They are also referred as diskettes.
- The data is read and write in floppy disk is using a device called FLOPPY DISC DRIVE.
- The long lit is provided for the read / writes head to access the disk.
- A hub in the centre is used for mounting the disk drive.
- A hole is used to sense index marking.
- The floppy disks are available in two sizes.
  - 5 ¼ inch (1.2 MB)
  - 3 ½ inch (1.44 MB)

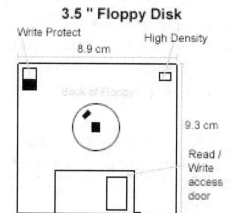

Advantages:
- Cheap in cost.
- Convenient offline storage for small computer users.

Disadvantages;
- Low storage capacity.
- A floppy disk drive device is required to use read/write data.

4. WRITE A DETAIL NOTE ON HARD DISK

- Hard disks are most popular secondary storage device.
- It supports the direct access of the data.
- It's a thin magnetic plate which is made of metal n both side coated with magnetic material.
- The disk is divided in many tracks & the data is store in both side of the disk.
- The disk pack consists of multiple disk plates.
- The disk drive pack has a separate read/write head for each disk surface.
- The disk drive consists of motor to rotate the disk pack about its axis at a speed of about 5400 revolution per minute.

- The drive also has a set of magnetic heads mounted on arms.
- The arm assembly is capable of moving in & out in radial direction.
- The hard disk drive has become the most indispensable secondary storage device in micro-computers.
- It is fast and speeds of less than 10 (ms) milliseconds are achievable.
- Storage capacity is large and it is not uncommon for micro-computers.

5. SHORT NOTE : CD-ROM

- CD-ROM (Compact Disk – Read Only Memory) is a non-erasable backing store which can hold large amounts of data.
- It's a shiny silver colour metal disk of 5 ¼ inch and the storage capacity about 650 megabytes.
- Large volume production is achieved by automated processes similar to that of audio compact disks.
- Many of today's micro-computers come with CD-ROM readers and as a result, CD-ROM is popularly used for distribution of software, digitized graphic images as well as Multi-Media material.
- Information is written on the disk surface by shining a laser beam.
- As a disk rotates the laser beam traces out a continuous spiral.
- It's known as WORM (Write Once Read Many) disk technology.
- The data can be read time and again but, once the data is stored, it cannot be erased or changed.

Advantages:
- Cost per bit is Low.
- Need not have any mechanical read/write heads to read/write data.
- Compact in size.
- Light weight

Disadvantages:
- Read only storage medium.
- Slower access speed than magnetic disk.

6. EXPLAIN IN BRIEF: DVD

- DVD (Digital Versatile Disk) is optical disk storage.
- Basically it is used for storing large amount of data including movies with high video & sound quality.
- Work on the same principle of CDROM.
- Data is recorded on each layer so that the storage capacity is become large.
- Total capacity of DVD is 8.5 GB

Advantages

- Larger capacity than CD.

Disadvantages:
- Expensive than CD.
- Damaged if not handled properly.

7.   EXPLAIN IN BRIEF: ZIP DISK

- It's a high capacity, removable magnetic disk which can be read or write by ZIP drive.
- It is similar to floppy disk except that much faster & larger capacity.
- Zip disks are available in two size namely 100 megabytes & 250 megabytes.

Advantages:
- Easy to use
- Large capacity than floppy disk.
- Faster than floppy disk
- Easy to carry.

Disadvantages:
- Expensive
- Data transfer between drive & computer is slow.

8.   SHORT NOTE: PEN DRIVE

- It consists of a small printed circuit board encased in a robust plastic or metal casing.
- It is easy to carry in pocket.
- It uses standard-A type connection which allows it to directly connect with the computer.
- It contains following components:
  - Male type-A USB connector-provides an interface to computer.
  - USB mass storage controller- provides liner interface to block oriented serial flash device.
  - NAND flash memory chip- stores data.
  - Crystal oscillator- controls device data.

ADVANTAGES:
- Portable in size.
- Can easily work with all new operating system.
- More reliable than floppy disk

DISADVANTAGES:
- Expensive than optical disk
- Do not provide protect mechanism.

9. <u>SHORT NOTE: BLUE RAY DISK</u>

- Blue-Ray disk is an optical disc storage media format.
- It was developed by blue-ray disc associations.
- It is mainly used to store high definition video and data.
- It has same dimensions as CD or DVD.
- The violet coloured laser is used to read and write the data.
- Because of its shorter wavelength more data can be stored than DVD format.
- Its storage capacity is 50 GB.

UNIT: 6 NUMBER SYSTEM

Introduction

- All digital computers store numbers, letters, and other characters in coded form.
- The code used to represent characters is the Binary Code – i.e. a code made up of bits called Binary Digits.
- Every character is represented by a string of "0s" and "1s" – the only digits found in the binary numbering system.

> "0" or "1" = bit (Binary Digit)
> 8 bits = 1 Byte (1 Character)
> 1024 Bytes = 1 KB (Kilo Bytes)
> 1024 KB = 1 MB (Mega Byte)
> 1024 MB = 1 GB (Giga Byte)
> 1024 GB= 1 TB (Terra Byte)

- When data is typed into a computer, the key board converts each key stroke into a binary character code. This code is then transmitted to the computer.
- When the computer transmits the data to the any device, each individual character is communicated in binary code. It is then converted back to the specific character while displaying or printing the data.

Number Systems

- Numbers earlier consisted of symbols like I for 1, II for 2, III for 3 etc. Each
- Symbol represented the same value irrespective of its position in the number.
- This approach is called an additive approach. As time passed positional numbering systems were developed. In such a system the number of symbols is few and they represent different values depending on the position they occupy.
- Now we know that numbers can be represented by arranging symbols in various positions.

Decimal Number System (Base 10)

- In the decimal system the successive positions to the left of the decimal point represent units, tens, hundreds, thousands etc. For example if we consider
- The number 7762, the digit 2 represents the number of units, 6 represents the number of tens, 7 the number of hundreds and 7 the number of thousands.
  (7 x 1000) + (7 x 100) + (6 x 10) + (2 x 1) = 7762
- Thus as we move one position to the left, the value of the digit increases by ten times. We can see that the position of the number affects its value.

- These kinds of number systems are therefore called positional number systems.
- In other words the number of symbols used to represent numbers in the system is called the base of that system. In short we can say that the value of each digit in the number system is determined by:
    - The digit itself
    - The position of the digit in the number itself
    - The base of the system.
- The Roman numbering system uses symbols like I, II, III, IV, V etc. To represent the decimal numbers 1, 2, 3, 4, and 5.
- As we can see this follows an additive approach and hence is not conductive to arithmetic.

Binary Number System (Base 2)

- We now come to a different number system – the Binary number system.
- This binary number system has a base of two, and the symbols used are "0" And "1".
- In this number system, as we move to the left the value of the digit will be two times greater than its predecessor. Thus the values of the places are: 64 32 16 8 4 2 1

Converting Decimal To Binary

- In conversion from decimal to any other number system, the steps to be followed are:
    - Divide the decimal number by the base of 2.
    - Note the remainder in one column and divide the quotient again with the base. Repeat this process until the quotient is reduced to a zero.

Example:
- The decimal number is 65

2	65	1
2	32	0
2	16	0
2	8	0
2	4	0
2	2	0
	1	

- The binary number of 65 is <u>1000001</u>

Converting Binary To Decimal

The decimal number of 100001 is

$$= (1*2^6)+(0*2^5)+(0*2^4)+(0*2^3)+(0*2^2)+(0*2^1)+(1*2^0)$$
$$= (1*64) + (0*32) + (0*16) + (0*8) + (0*4) + (0*2) + (1 * 1)$$

$$= 64 + 0 + 0 + 0 + 0 + 0 + 1$$

$$= 65$$

- The decimal number of 1000001 is <u>65</u>

Octal Number System (Base 8)

- A commonly used positional system is the Octal System. The octal system has a base of 8.
- The values increase from left to right as 1, 8, 64, 512, 4096,....

Converting Decimal To Octal

- In conversion from decimal to any other number system, the steps to be followed are:
  - ○ Divide the decimal number by the base of the 8.

Example:
- The decimal number is 224

8	224	0
8	28	4
8	3	3

- The octal number of 224 is <u>340</u>

Converting Octal To Decimal

- The octal number is 340
- $= (3*8^2)+(4*8^1)+(0*8^0)$
- $= (3*64) + (4*8) + (0*1)$
- $= 192 + 32 + 0$
- $= 224$
- The decimal number of 340 is <u>224</u>

Converting Binary Octal

000	0
001	1
010	2
011	3
100	4
101	5
110	6
111	7

Converting from Binary to Octal

- The binary number must be divided into groups of three from the octal point – to the right in case of the fractional portion and to the left in case of the integer portion. Each group can then be replaced with their octal equivalent.
- Example
- Binary 101010101010100

  <u>101</u> <u>010</u> <u>101</u> <u>010</u> <u>100</u>

    5   2   5   2   4
- So, <u>52524</u> is the Octal equivalent of binary 101010101010100

Converting Octal to Binary

- Each octal digit is replaced with the appropriate 'triple' of binary digits.

  e.g. 65

      6 5

    110 101
- The binary equivalent of the Octal number 65 is <u>110101</u>

Hexadecimal Number System (Base 16)

- There is another commonly used positional system, hexadecimal system.
- The hexadecimal system has a base of 16, so the value increases from left to right as 1, 16, 256, 65536,. . . .
- We need to keep a simple table in mind before we attempt any conversion from hexadecimal or vice-versa.

Converting Decimal To HexaDecimal

- In conversion from decimal to any other number system, the steps to be followed are:
  - Divide the decimal number by the base of 16.

Example:

- The decimal number is 370

16	370	2
16	23	7
16	1	1
	0	

- The hexadecimal number of 370 is <u>172</u>

Converting Hexadecimal To Decimal

The hexadecimal number 172

    $= (1*16^2) + (7*16^1) + (2*16^0)$

    $= (1*256) + (7*16) + (2*1)$

    $= 256+112+2$

= 370
- The decimal number of 172 is <u>370</u>

Converting Binary to Hexadecimal

- Each hexadecimal digit is represented by 4 binary digits.

Binary Hexadecimal

Binary	Hexadecimal
0000	0
0001	1
0010	2
0011	3
0100	4
0101	5
0110	6
0111	7
1000	8
1001	9
1010	A
1011	B
1100	C
1101	D
1110	E
1111	F

- To convert a binary number to its hexadecimal equivalent we split the quantity into groups of four onwards, as before.
- Each of this group of four is directly converted into their hexadecimal equivalent.
- We may add zeros to the left of the number if necessary.
- example

  Binary 10101011000010

  <u>0010</u> <u>1010</u> <u>1100</u> <u>0010</u>

     2   A   C   2

- So, the hexadecimal equivalent of binary 10101011000010 will be <u>2AC2</u>

Converting Hexadecimal to Binary

- The conversion from hexadecimal to binary consists of writing off the binary

Equivalent of each hexadecimal digit in groups of four.

- e.g.
  Hexadecimal 1901A0412C
  <u>0001</u> <u>1001</u> <u>0000</u> <u>0001</u> <u>1010</u> <u>0000</u> <u>0100</u> <u>0001</u> <u>0010</u> <u>1100</u>
    1   9   0   1   A   0   4   1   2   C
- Thus the required binary number can be written as:
  <u>11001000000011010000001000001001011100</u>

Converting Hexadecimal to Octal

- Write 4 digit binary numbers for each hexadecimal.
- Arrange the entire number sequence into group of 3 bit section.
- If any bit is missing add 0 on leftmost section.
- Now write down octal equivalent of each 3 bit section.
- Example:
- The hexadecimal number is 2A35.

  2 A 3 5
  0010 1010 0011 0101
  <u>000</u> <u>010</u> <u>101</u> <u>000</u> <u>110</u> <u>101</u>
    0   2   5   0   6   5
-       The octal number is <u>25065</u>

Converting Octal to Hexadecimal

- Write 3 digit binary number for each octal.
- Arrange the entire number sequence into group of 4 bit section.
- If any bit is missing add 0 on leftmost section.
- Now write down hexadecimal equivalent of each 4 bit section.
- Example:
- The octal number is 25065.

  2 5 0 6 5
  010 101 000 110 101
  <u>0010</u> <u>1010</u> <u>0011</u> <u>0101</u>
    2   A   3   5

The hexadecimal number is <u>2A35</u>

Binary Arithmetic

- All the arithmetic operations are possible in binary numbering system like addition, subtraction, multiplication and division All the Arithmetic operations are done in binary number system are explained as under:

Addition

- For binary addition the following rules of binary addition are to be considered:
  - $0 + 0 = 0$
  - $0 + 1 = 1$
  - $1 + 0 = 1$
  - $1 + 1 = 0$ (carry 1 to the next column to the left)
  - $1 + 1 + 1 = 1$ (carry 1 to the next column)
- e.g. 1 Add two binary numbers 11011 and 111
- Carry   1 1 1 1

```
         1 0 1 1 1
       +     1 1 1
       ─────────────
       1 0 0 0 1 0 (Answer)
```

Subtraction

- Though there are other methods of performing subtraction, we will consider the method of subtraction know as complementary subtraction.
- This is a more efficient method of subtraction while using electronic circuits. We will be following three steps to perform subtraction:
  - Find the complement of the number you are subtracting.
  - To the complement of the number we obtained in step 1, we add the number we are subtracting from.
  - If there is a carry of 1 add the carry to the result of the addition else re complement the sum and attach a negative sign.
- How do we find the complement of a binary number ? We have to invert all the bits. e.g. Number Complement
  10001101 01110010
  00101010 11010101
- Consider the following example of subtraction:
  e.g. 1
  1010101 – 1001100
- Step-1. Find the complement of 1001100
          0110011

- **Step-2. Add the number you are subtracting from**

  Carry 1 1 1 0 1 1 1

       1 0 1 0 1 0 1

   +0 1 1 0 0 1 1

  ───────────

     0 0 0 1 0 0 0

               + 1 (Continue since there is a carry of 1)

  ───────────

     0 0 0 1 0 0 1 (Answer)

e.g. 2

101100 – 11100101

- **Step-1. Find the complement of 11100101**

  00011010

- **Step-2. Add the number you are subtracting from**

  Carry 0 1 1 1

       0 0 1 0 1 1 0 0

   +0 0 0 1 1 0 1 0

  ───────────

    0 1 0 0 0 1 1 0

- **Step-3. Since there is no carry we are complement the result**

  10111001

 attach a negative sign

- - 10111001 (Answer)

Multiplication

- Multiplication
- Multiplication in binary follows the same rules that are followed in the decimal system. The table to be remembered is:
- 0 x 0 = 0
- 0 x 1 = 0
- 1 x 0 = 0
- 1 x 1 = 1
- e.g.

  1010 * 1001

         1010

     x 1001

  ───────────

```
            1010
            0000
            0000
            1010
       _____

       101101 0
```

- The answer is (1011010)

Division

- Table for binary division is given as under:
- $0 / 1 = 1$
- $1 / 1 = 1$
- The steps for binary division are:
  - Start from the left of the dividend.
  - Perform subtraction in which the divisor is subtracted from the dividend
  - If subtraction is possible put a 1 in the quotient and subtract the divisor from the corresponding digits of the dividend else put a 0 in the quotient
  - Bring down the next digit to the right of the remainder.
  - Execute step 2 till there are no more digits left to strating down from the dividend.
- e.g.
- 100001 / 110

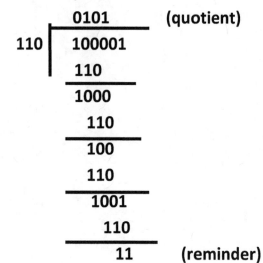

Unit Of Information (Codes)

- Most computers do not represent characters as pure binary numbers.
- They use a coded version of true binary to represent letters and special symbols as well as decimal numbers.
- Coding of characters has been standardized to enable transfer of data between computers.
- Codes used are:
    - BCD
    - ASCII
    - EBCDIC

BCD

- BCD stands for Binary Coded Decimal.
- BCD code is one of the early computer codes.
- It is based on the idea of converting each digit of a decimal number into its binary equivalent rather than converting the entire decimal into binary form.
- All decimal digits are represented in BCD by 4 bit.
- Each decimal digit is independently converted into a 4 bit binary number & so the conversion process is very easy.
- 4 bit BCD can be used to represents only decimal numbers because 4 bits are insufficient to represent various characters.
- By using 4 bit BCD only 16 possible characters are represented.
- So the BCD code was extended from 6-bit code and it is possible to represent 64 characters.

ASCII

- ASCII stands for American Standard Code for Information Interchange.
- In this form of representation, each character (which includes alphabets, digits and symbols) is assigned a particular pattern of bits.
- For example, A is represented as binary 1000012, B as 10000102 and so on.
- The standard ASCII character set uses 7 bits and can be used to represent 128 different characters.
- It uses one extra parity bit for parity check.
- Other forms of ASCII codes use an extra bit to extend the representation to 256 characters.
- However, characters represented from binary are not universally agreed upon.
- The most popular form is the set used by IBM.
- ASCII is commonly used to exchange data between data processing and communication systems.

EBCDIC

- EBCDIC stands for Extended Binary Coded Decimal Interchange Code.
- It uses 8 bits and can represent 256 distinct characters.
- It also uses one extra parity bit for parity check.
- The EBCDIC code is used in IBM mainframe models and other similar machines.
- Electronic Circuits are available to transform characters from ASCII to EBCDIC and vice-versa and can also be achieved using computer programs.

UNICODE

- With the onset of globalization through Internet, there emerged a need to Cater for data interchange of the more common languages of the different nationalities like Chinese, Korea and Japanese.
- ASCII, EBCDIC and other forms of representation proved insufficient.
- The Unicode/ISO 10646 standard was devised to overcome this problem.
- The 16 bits used by Unicode can represent 65536 symbols, one extra parity bit for parity check, which is more than enough to represent all the worlds written characters.
- Although Unicode solves the problem of multi-language data representation, it is not the perfect solution as there remain issues to be addressed.
- Problems include the wastage of storage space, time needed for data transmission and the lack of support of current operating systems.
- Furthermore, Unicode does not guarantee a particular sort order.

Parity Check

- A parity check is a technique to detect the correctness of characters transmitted.
- For each character transmitted, a bit knows as the parity bit is added.
- In an Even Parity System, a parity bit is added such that the total number of '1's, inclusive of the parity bit, is even.
- In an Odd Parity System, the total number of '1' bits transmitted must be odd.
- The parity check is not fool proof. It will fail when an even number of bits were incorrectly received.
- This cannot be recognized by this system. That if they are incorrectly received or not.

UNIT:7 LANGUAGES, OPERATING SYSTEM & SOFTWARE PACKAGES

Introduction

- A computer can only do what a programmer asks it to do.
- To perform a particular task programmer writes a sequence, called the program.
- An instruction command given to the computer to perform a certain specified operation on the given data.
- Now as we know only human languages and computer knows only machine language, we need some media through which we can communicate with the computer.
- So we can complete our desired task. That media is Language.
- Languages are tools human can use to communicate with the hardware of a computer system.
- Each language has a systematic method of using symbols of that language.
- In English, this method is given by the rules of grammar.
- Similarly, the symbols of particular one computer language must also be used as per set of rules which are known as the "Syntax" of that language, the language which you are using.
- Computer Languages can be classified into three broad categories:

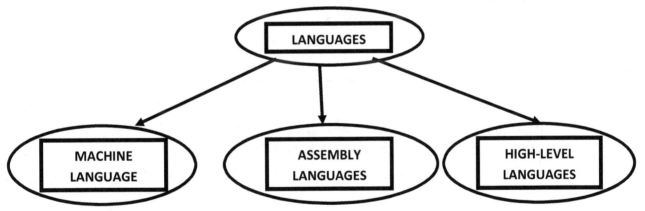

1. WHAT IS MACHINE LANGUAGE?

- Computer programs are written using many different computer Languages but the language which is understood by the computer without translating program is called machine language.
- Machine language is normally written as string of binary 1s and 0s.
- A machine language instruction has two part format.

OPCODE (OPERATION CODE)	OPERAND (ADDRESS)

- The 1st part is the operation code which tells the computer what function to be performed.
- The 2nd part is the operand which tells the computer where to find & store data to be manipulated.
- So each instruction tells the computer what operation to perform & the length & location of the data field which are involved in the operation.

Advantages

- Programs can be executed immediately upon completion because it doesn't require any translation.
- Now extra storage space is needed.
- Programmer has complete control over the performance of the hardware.

Disadvantage

- Tedious to program
- Difficult to program
- Difficult to modify
- Time consuming to code
- Error prone
- Operation codes have to be memorised
- Assignment of memory is done by programmer
- Time consuming for development
- Programs development are machine dependent
- Preparation of programs was slow and costly.

2. EXPLAIN ASSEMBLY LANGUAGE.

- Assembly language is a language which allows instruction & storage location to be represented by letters & symbols, instead of number.
- A program written in an assembly language is called assembly language program or symbolic program.
- Assembly language was introduced in 1952.
- Machine language was tedious to code and errors were expected to arise in bulk.
- To solve these problems mnemonic codes and symbolic addresses were developed.
- It allows using alphanumeric mnemonic codes instead of numeric code for the instructions in instruction set. For example using ADD instead of 1110 or 14 to add.

- The storage locations are to be represented in the form of alphanumeric addresses instead of numeric address.
- Format of assembly language is similar to machine language:

MNEMONIC CODE	SYMBOLIC ADDRESS

Example of Assembly language instruction:
- This instruction adds value of NUM1 to the AX (Accumulator Register).
- The symbolic language made program writing so much easier for the Programmers but it must be translated into machine code before being used for operation.
- The translation is actually done by a special translating program.

Assembler
- Assembler is a special program (translator) which translates symbolic operation codes into machine codes, and symbolic address is addressed into an actual machine address.

Advantage
- Easier to use, code and understand.
- Easier to correct error.
- Easier to modify.
- No worry about addresses.
- Easily relocatable.
- Efficiency of machine language.
- Can use Macros (Macro is a bunch of instruction referred as a single name)

Disadvantage
- Machine depended.
- Programs have to be translated before execution.
- Translation of programs takes up time.
- Knowledge of hardware is required.
- Additional storage area needed for the source programs and object code.

Examples of Assembly Language
- Microsoft Assembly Language (MASM), Turbo Assembler

3. WRITE A NOTE ON HIGH LEVEL LANGUAGE.
- The machine language & assembly language requires a good knowledge of internal structure of computer.
- The both languages are machine dependent & it is difficult to solve error.
- To remove this limitation the high level language are introduced.

- The high level languages machine independent so it can be easily ported & executed on any computer.
- The high level language programs do not require any knowledge of internal structure of computer so the programmer concentrate on the logic of problem rather than internal structure of computer.
- It enables the programmer to write instructions using English words & familiar mathematical symbols & expression so the program makes easier to code & understand.
- It requires a translator program to convert high level program into machine language.

Compiler
- Compiler is a special program (translator) which translates high level programs into machine codes.

Advantages:
- Machine independent.
- Easier to learn, use and understand.
- Easier to correct error.
- Easier to maintain.
- Less time & efforts.
- Easily relocatable.
- Program preparation cost is low.
- Few errors.

Disadvantages:
- Less flexible.
- Lower efficiency.
- Require more time & storage space.

4. SHORT NOTE: ASSEMBLER

- A computer can directly execute only machine language programs so the assembly language program must be converted into its equivalent machine language program before can be executed.
- This translation is done with the help of a translator program which is known as assembler.
- Assembler is a special program (translator) which translates symbolic operation codes into machine codes, and symbolic address is addressed into an actual machine address.

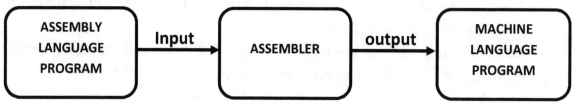

- As shown in figure that the input to assembler is the assembly language program (source program) and the output is the machine language program (object program).
- Assembler translates each assembly language instruction into equivalent machine language instruction.
- There is <u>one to one correspondence</u> between the assembly language instructions of source program & the machine language instruction of its equivalent object program.
- In case of assembly language program the computer not only has to run the program but also must first run assembler program to translate the original assembly language program into machine language program.
- So the computer has to spend more time in getting desired answer.

5.   <u>WRITE A NOTE ON COMPILER</u>

- A computer can directly execute only machine language programs.
- So the high level language program must be converted into its equivalent machine language program before can be executed.
- This translation is done with the help of a translator program which is known as compiler.
- A compiler is a translator program which translates a high level language program into equivalent machine language program.
- The process of translating is shown in below figure:

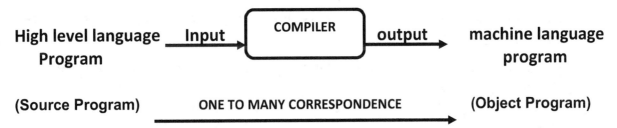

High level language Program   Input   COMPILER   output   machine language program

(Source Program)   ONE TO MANY CORRESPONDENCE   (Object Program)

- As shown in figure that the input to compiler is the high level language program (source program) and the output is the machine language program (object program).
- High level language instructions are macro instructions.
- The compiler translates each high level language instruction into set of machine language instructions rather than a single machine language instruction.
- There is <u>one to many correspondence</u> between high level language instructions of source program into equivalent object program.
- During the translation the source program is <u>only translates not executed.</u>

- A compiler can translates only those source programs which have written in the language for which compiler is designed.
- A compiler can also detect & indicates the syntax errors during the compilation process but cannot able to detect logical errors.

6. WRITE A NOTE ON INTERPRETER.

- An interpreter is another type of translator which is used for translating program written using high level languages.
- It takes one statement of high level language, translates into machine language & immediately executes the resulting machine language instructions.
- The main difference between compiler & interpreter is that compiler can translates the entire code but not involve in execution.

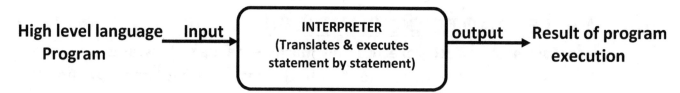

High level language Program →Input→ INTERPRETER (Translates & executes statement by statement) →output→ Result of program execution

- As shown in figure that the input to an interpreter is a source program & the output is the result of an execution program.
- Interpreter translates & executes a high level language program statement-by-statement.
- A program statement is reinterpreted every time it is encountered during program execution.
- The main advantage of interpreter is that interpreter makes it easier & faster to correct programs.
- The main disadvantage is that interpreter is slower than compilers when running a finished program.

7. WHAT IS OPERATING SYSTEM?

- An operating system is a software program that provides an interface between user & the computer and manages thousands of applications.
- It's a collection of system software that co-ordinates between the hardware, provides a platform for software to run on.
- An operating system is an integrated set of programs that the resources (the CPU, memory, I/O devices etc) of computer system & provides an interface to the user to run the machine.
- The main two primary objective of operating system are:
  - Making a computer system convenient to use

o Managing the resources of a computer system

1) PROCESS MANAGEMENT
- o The process management of OS taking care about the creation & deletion of user & system process, providing mechanism for process synchronization & process communication.

2) MEMORY MANAGEMENT
- o The memory management of OS taking care about the allocation & deallocation of memory space to the various programs in need of this resource.

3) FILE MANAGEMENT
- o The file management of OS is taking care about the file related activities such as creation, storing, retrieving, naming, sharing & organization of files.

4) SECURITY
- o The security model of OS protects the resources & information of a computer system against destruction & unauthorized access.

5) COMMAND INTERPRETATION
- o This model taking care of interpreting user commands & directing the system resources to handle the requests.

8. WHAT IS BATCH OPERATING SYSTEM.

- In Batch operating system, data is collected over a period of time and the processing of the data is deferred to a later time.
- This approach was used very commonly in the past when punch cards served as data storage media and is used as input into the computer system for processing.
- In batch processing, the data have first to be captured, normally as a form of source documents, like time cards, or alternatively, by RJE (Remote Job Entry) where data is gathered through remote terminals.
- The data will then be transmitted to the computer or the source document will be physically transported to the data centre where transcription (conversion of source document data into machine readable form) is performed.
- The data is processed by the computer and the resulting output is given to the users.
- Batch processing is suitable in application where there are large amounts of data and when the turnaround times are not critical.

- As data are transcribed into machine readable form before submitting for processing, the speed of processing is therefore determined by the computer and not by the operator.
- Payroll processing is suitable for batch processing as it is only performed on a regular basis. (for example every month)

ADVANTAGES:
- Less complicated.
- After input process is over, while processing is going on, user can attend other jobs.

DISADVANTAGES:
- Long turnaround time.
- Access to one is not possible.
- Difficult to provide priority scheduling.
- Not convenient for program development.

9. EXPLAIN REALTIME OPERATIN SYSTEM.

- Real-Time systems are always on-line but on-line systems need not be real-time systems.
- However, further constraints are placed in terms of response time and availability of the system.
- By definition, a real time system receive data and process it quickly enough to produce output which can be used to control or affect the outcome of an ongoing activity of process.
- In general, real-time systems handle small volumes of data at any one time and the turnaround time is critical.
- Feedback is essential in real-time systems so that processing can keep pace with external factors.
- Most real-time systems are used in mission critical application like process control and therefore, reliability and availability is of paramount importance.
- Missile guidance systems are examples of real-time systems.
- Control signals are sent to the fins of the missile to correct any deviations.

Advantages
- Error messages are immediate
- Source documents are available at the time the error occurs.
- Faster than on-line systems.

Disadvantages
- Direct access devices have to be used.
- Elaborate controls and backup procedures to guard against unwarranted access to the system.
- Control checks are difficult since updating occurs at the time of processing.

10. EXPLAIN TIME SHARING OPERATING SYSTEM

- Time-sharing is a mechanism that allows the many users to use a computer system in such a way that each user is given the impression that they use their own system.
- It has many user terminals simultaneously connected to the same computer.
- Using these terminals multiple users can simultaneously work on the system.
- The multiprogramming feature allows multiple programs to simultaneously reside in the memory.
- The special scheduling algorithm used in a time-sharing system.
- In this very short period of CPU time allocates to each user process.
- When the CPU is allocated to user process, the process will use CPU until the allocate time slice is expires or the execution process is over during this time period.

Features:
- The processing time is divided among various programs in time slices.
- Each program is given control of CPU only for time slice turn by turn.

Advantages:
- Reduce CPU idle time
- Provides advantages of quick response time.
- Offers good computing facility to small users.

11. EXPLAIN: MULTIPROGRAMMING OPERATING SYSTEM

- Multiprogramming is the name given to the interleaved execution of two or more different & independent programs by the same computer.
- In this more than one program in main memory at a same time.
- In multiprogramming operating system two or more programs are resides in the main memory and it execute them concurrently.
- In this operating system the CPU can allocate time to several programs instead of remaining idle when one program is busy with I/O operations the another program is ready to utilize the CPU.

ADVANTAGES:
- Many programs can run simultaneously.
- Time is not wasted.
- Maximum use of resources.

DISADVANTAGES:
- Required large memory.
- Required memory protection.

- Job of resources management & memory management increases.

12. EXPLAIN: MULTIPROCESSING OPERATING SYSTEM

- It is the type of operating system that makes the use of more than one CPU.
- The term multiprocessing describe interconnected two or more CPUs that have an ability to execute several programs simultaneously.
- In such system, instruction from different independent programs can be processed at same instant of time by different CPU.

ADVANTAGES:
- It improves the performance of computer.
- Less turnaround time.
- In case of failure of one CPU other can take over without any loss.

DISADVANTAGES:
- Large main memory required.
- Expensive
- Design of the system makes time consuming process.

13. EXPLAIN TYPES OF SOFTWARE PACKAGES

- The software is set of programs, procedure and associated documents which describe the programs and how they are used.
- On the base of task performed by software it can be divided in following tasks.
- WORD PROCESSING SOFTWARE :
  - It enables you to make use of computer system for creating, editing, and viewing, formatting, storing, retrieving & printing documents.
- SPREAD SHEET SOFTWARE:
  - Spreadsheet software is a numeric data analysis tool, which allows us to create kinds of computerised ledger.
  - Provides a predefined sheet which contains rows and columns.
- DATABASE SOFTWARE
  - A database is a collection of related data stored & treated as a unit for information retrieval purpose.
  - Database software is a set of one or more programs which enables us to create a database, maintain it, and organize it.
- GRAPHICS SOFTWARE:
  - Graphic software enables you to use a computer system for creating, editing, viewing, storing, retrieving and printing designs, drawings, pictures, graphs.
- PERSONAL ASSITANCE SOFTWARE:

- o It allows you to use personal computers for storing & retrieving your personal information & planning & managing schedules, contacts, inventory & important items.
- PRESENTATION SOFTWARE:
  - o It allows you to provide the tools which help you to develop a presentation on specific subject.
- ANIMATION/VIDEO/SOUND PACKAGE:
  - o Provides the different kinds of application that allows you to generate animation, watching or creating videos, playing or producing sound data.

14. EXPLAIN: ONLINE OPERATING SYSTEM

- In an On-Line system, the terminal used by the operator is connected to the main computer so that the operator can interact with the computer in a conversational mode.
- It is used in applications requiring fast response from the computer.
- There are some benefits by allowing users to communicate with the computer on-line.
- Error checking can be performed by the computer when data entry is carried out.
- The operator can be informed of the error so that immediate correction can be made.
- On-Line queries can be performed to allow immediate retrieval of information.
- The nature of on-line systems allows centralization of information, fast data retrieval immediate file updates and improved customer services.
- Limited validation checks at the terminal increases the accuracy of input.
- However, the cost of implementation such a system is much more than the batch system.
- Furthermore, as the terminals may be located remotely from the main computer site, security aspects of implementation must receive special considerations.
- Aspects which should be incorporated are
  - o Security of access to facilities
  - o Security of data files
  - o Audit trial – maintaining a record of all actions that have been carried out to any data

UNIT:8 TECHNOLOGIES AND VIRUS

Introduction

- Emerging technologies are contemporary advances and innovation in various fields of technology.
- Various converging technologies have emerged in the technological convergence of different systems evolving towards similar goals.
- Convergence can refer to previously separate technologies such as voice (and telephony features), data (and productivity applications) and video that now share resources and interact with each other, creating new efficiencies.
- Emerging technologies are those technical innovations which represent progressive developments within a field for competitive advantage

1.   SHORT NOTE: GIS

- A GIS (Geographic Information System) is a tool that uses for the answer of the geographic question
- A GIS integrates hardware, software, and data for capturing, managing, analyzing, and displaying all forms of geographically referenced information.
- GIS allows us to view, understand, question, interpret, and visualize data in many ways that reveal relationships, patterns, and trends in the form of maps, globes, reports, and charts.
- A GIS helps you answer questions and solve problems by looking at your data in a way that is quickly understood and easily shared.
- GIS technology can be integrated into any enterprise information system framework.
- By using GIS tool, user can arrange and display the data about places on the earth in variety of ways including maps, charts and tables.
- We can store, analyze and manage the data about places on the earth with the help of GIS tool.
- User can zoom in and out of maps, charts and tables freely and study in details.
- By using GIS tool, we can create maps, charts and tables and also we can solve the complicated problems and develop the effective solutions.

- GIS allows automatic determination of the relationships between maps & can create a new map of those relationships.
- GIS allows the relating of multiple data bases using common geographic locations and allows powerful analyses of widely disparate data.

COMPONENTS OF GIS
There are 5 types components of a GIS like
- Hardware
- Software
- Data
- People
- Method

GIS IS USED FOR
- Allows to find the geographical locations
- Maintain an up-to-date planning & environmental inventory.
- Create a library of regional & community infrastructure resources.
- Plan major facilities and services
- Facilities management.
- Define natural resource areas.

GIS used in:
- In Agriculture
- In Business
- In Electric-Gas
- In Environment
- In Forestry
- In Military
- In Land Planning
- In Site Planning
- In Water Industry

2. SHORT NOTE: GPS
- GPS means Global Positioning System and it is a satellite based navigation system.
- GIS is a system that can provide a position at any point on the Earth's surface to a very high degree of accuracy.
- GPS provides the position information of the earth.
- GPS is a system that measures the distances from the satellites that are in path around the Earth.

- By knowing the distance from the satellites, it is possible to calculate the position on the Earth's surface.
- The satellite sends all the timing and position information to the receiver so the receiver knows when the message was sent and also the receiver is able
- To calculate the distance from the satellite about their position.
- The satellite contains an atomic clock so that the satellite sends the timing information to the receiver that is very accurate.
- The satellite uses their own power through their solar panels and these extend to about 17 feet and it provides 700 watts power.
- Each satellite is in circular orbit around the earth and it sends the data on two frequencies like L1 (1600 MHz) and L2 (1300 MHz).
- A GPS (Global Positioning System) is the satellite-based system that provides accurate information about position, speed and time of the earth.
- There are 24 satellites in GPS that orbits the earth at a height of about 12000 miles.
- Each of this satellite are constantly moving and making two complete orbits in less than 24 hours.
- The speed of satellite is 7000 miles per hour.
- A GPS contains 3 types of segments like User, Control and Space.
- User segment changes according to the requirements of application but
- Control and Space segments do not change for all applications.

GPS APPLICATIONS:
  - Navigation
  - Agriculture
  - Space Shuttle
  - Tourism
  - Air Traffic Control
  - Surveying and mapping
  - Remote sensing
  - military

3. SHORT NOTE: CDMA
- CDMA stands for Code Division Multiple Accesses.
- CDMA is a spread spectrum technology that allows many users to occupy the same time & frequency allocations in a given space.
- CDMA assigns unique codes to each user to differentiate it from other in the same spectrum.
- Its platform on which 2G & 3G advanced services are built.

- The foremost application of CDMA technology is digital cellular phone technology operating in 800MHz and 1.9HZ PCS bands.
- After the speech the codec converts voice into digital, CDMA spread the voice stream over the full 1.25MHz bandwidth of the CDMA channel, coding each stream separately so it can be decoded at the receiving end.'
- The rape of spreading signal is known as the 'chip rate' as each bit in the spreading single is known as 'chip'.
- All voice conversations use the full bandwidth at the same time.
- One bit from each conversation is multiplied into 128 bits by the spreading techniques.

STANDARD OF CDMA:
- There are number of standards that employs CDMA for instance, IS-95A, IS-95B,CDMA-1 etc.
- CDMA-1 describes a complete wireless system.
- It represents the end-to-end wireless system and all the necessary specifications that administer its operation.
- CDMA provides a collection of related services including fixed wired, wireless local loop and cellular within the personal communication services family

ADVANTAGES:
- Provides good quality & low power consumption
- Avoid interceptions.
- Require fewer cell sites than GSM
- This technology provides good resistance to fading problems.

4. SHORT NOTE: GSM
- GSM stands for Global System For Mobile communication.
- GSM is the most popular standard for mobile phones in the world.
- Its promoter, the GSM association, estimates that 80% of the global mobile market uses the standard.
- GSM is used by over 3 billion people across more than 212 countries.
- Its ubiquity makes international roaming very common between mobile phone operators, enabling subscribers to use their phones in many parts of the world.
- GSM differs from its predecessors in both signalling & speech channels are digital & thus it is considered as 2G mobile phone system.
- The GSM standard has been an advantage to the both consumers and also network operators.
- GSM pioneered a low cost alternative to voice calls, the short message service(SMS) which is now supported on other mobile standard as well.

- Another advantage of GSM is that the standard includes one worldwide emergency telephone number, 112.
- This makes it easier for international travellers to connect to emergency services without knowing the local emergency numbers.
- There are 5 different cell sizes in a GSM network: macro, micro, pico, femto and umbrella cells.
- The coverage area of each cell varies according to the implementation environment.

5. WRITE A NOTE ON FOLLOWING COMMUNICATION DEVICES:

MODEM

- Converting digital signal into analog is called modulation and the reverse process that is converting analog signal into digital signals is called demodulation.
- The word "MODEM" comes from the term modulation-demodulation
- Computer can store & transmit data digitally while our telephone lines can transmit data in analog signals.
- When an analog facility is used for data communication between two digital devices, two modems are required, one near each digital device.
- The analog signal is transmitted through the telephone line which is converted into digital by modem.
- To connect a computer network that are at distant location by using telephone line then modems must be used at both ends to do the modulation & demodulations.
- The modem is an essential piece of hardware for any application in which two digital devices want to communicate over an analog transmission channel.
- Different capacity modems are available according to different data transfer rate.

INFRARED

- Infrared are widely used for short-range communications.
- Distance is about to only 1 meters range.
- Remote controls used on television, VCRs and stereos all used in infrared communications.
- They are directional, cheap and easy to build but do not pass through solid objects.
- Infrared is used for indoor wireless LANs.
- Two types of infrared given below:

- Point to point
  - Point to point systems requires direct alignment between devices.
  - Many laptop systems and PDAS use point-to-point transmission.
- Broadcast
  - Broadcast infrared transmissions use a spread signal.
  - One broadcast in all directions instead of a direct beam.
  - This help to reduce the problems of proper alignment & obstructions.
  - It allows multiple receivers of a signal.

BLUETOOTH

- Bluetooth is the technology using short range radio links, intended to replace the cables connecting portable/fixed electronic devices.
- By using Bluetooth the users can have all mobile and fixed computer devices can be totally coordinated.
- The standard defines a uniform structure for a wide range of devices to communicate with each other and minimal user efforts.
- This technology offers wireless access to LANs, PSTN, the mobile phone network and the internet.
- Bluetooth technology use license-free 2.4GHz frequency band.
- You can connect wireless device up to 10 meter.
- The main advantage of Bluetooth is it can able to simultaneously handle both data & voice transmissions.
- Bluetooth is a radio based wireless technology which allows devices to share information over a maximum range of 10 meters.
- It enables computers, phones and the other peripherals to communicate with one another without cables.
- Provides more security, flexibility and less power consumptions.

ADVANTAGES:
- Less power consumptions.
- Enhances user's experience.
- Voice conferencing & video clips on cell phone is possible.
- Connect devices without using cable.

WI-FI
- Wi-Fi stands for wireless fidelity.
- It is used to define any of the wireless technology in the IEEE 802.11.
- It is useful to get internet access.
- It's a wireless way to handle networking.
- It is also known as 802.11 networking or wireless networking.

- It provides the facility to connect computers anywhere in your home office without need of physical connection.
- Wi-Fi allows connecting the computers within up to 100 feet area.
- Wi-Fi network uses radio technologies called IEEE 802.11 which provides fast, secure & reliable wireless connectivity.
- Wi-Fi setup contains one or more access points & one or more clients.
- The Wi-Fi standard leaves connection criteria & roaming totally open to the client.
- Wi-Fi transmit in the air, it has some properties as a non-switched wired Ethernet network therefore collisions can occur.
- Wi-Fi cannot do collision detection.
- Wi-Fi network can be used to connect computer to each other to the internet & wired networks.
- Wi-Fi networks operate in the unlicensed 2.4 and 5 GHZ radio bands.

ADVANTAGES:
- Allows LANs to be deployed without cabling.
- Allows you to connect any place within up to 100feet area.
- Contains one more access points and connect with one or more clients.
- Wi-Fi products are widely available in market.
- DISADVANTAGES:
- Limited range.
- Power consumption is higher than Bluetooth.
- Wi-Fi devices do not have channels to avoid interference.

6. WHAT IS COMPUTE VIRUS?EXPLAIN TYPES OF VIRUS

- A computer virus is a program that can copy itself & infect a computer without permission or knowledge of the user.
- It's a small piece of software that damages the real programs.
- A virus can only spread from one computer to another when it host is taken to the uninfected computer by internet or removable medium such as CD or USB.
- In computers virus is a program that replicates to another program, computer boot sector or document.
- Virus can be transmitted as attachments to an e-mail or downloaded file or be present on CD.
- The virus is classified in main five types.
- FILE INFECTORS
  - o It infects program files.

- Normally infect executable files such as .COM or .EXT files.
- Some virus can infect any program when the program is requested for execution such as .SYS, .OVL, .PRG and .MNU files.
- Many of this virus are memory resident.

- **BOOT SECTOR VIRUS**
  - This virus infects executable code found in certain system areas on a disk.
  - They attached to the DOS boot sector or the master boot record on hard disks.
  - Boot sector virus attaches themselves to the boot record information and activate when user attempt to start up form disk.
  - This virus are always memory resident.

- **MULTI-PARTITE VIRUSES:**
  - Known as polypartite.
  - They infect both boot records and program files.
  - This virus is difficult to repair.
  - If the boot area is cleaned, but the files are not than boot area infected again.

- **MACRO VIRUSES:**
  - These are the most common virus and they tend to do the least damage.
  - These types of virus infect data files such as it can infect your word document and insert unwanted words or phrases.
  - Ex. W97M, Melissa

- **STEALTH VIRUSES:**
  - These viruses use certain techniques to avoid detection.
  - They may either redirect disk head to read another sector instead of the one which they are reside or alter the reading of infected files.

7. PROTECTION FROM VIRUS.

- You can protect system against virus with a few simple steps.
  - Write protected your floppy when suing them on the other computer.
  - Remove floppy while booting.
  - Install software from original write- protected disks.
  - Use secure operating system like UNIX
  - Do not install pirated software.
  - Scans files downloaded from the internet.
  - Scan your system regularly if you continue using internet.
  - Use good antivirus program to scan removable devices as well as system.
  - Do not open attachments who contains an executable files.
  - Do not open spam or junk mails
  - Prepare a reuse disk with critical system files. Probably it should bootable.

www.ingramcontent.com/pod-product-compliance
Lightning Source LLC
LaVergne TN
LVHW081803050326
832903LV00027B/2075